BUDDHISM

KEY STAGE 1

By

Jing Yin
Ken Hudson

Published by
Buddhist Education Foundation (UK)
Registered Charity No.: 1073008
2000

First published in Great Britain in 2000
by
Buddhist Education Foundation (UK)

This is a complimentary Buddhist textbook,
which can be obtained from
The Buddhist Education Foundation (UK)
BCM 9459, London WC1N 3XX
United Kingdom

WWW.buddhisteducation.co.uk
info@buddhisteducation.co.uk

Registered Charity No.: 1073008

ISBN 0 9536928 0 9

Illustrated by Yanfeng Liu
Produced by media 2000

PREFACE

The present publication constitutes the first out of four textbooks on Buddhism devised for children between five and seven years of age. The primary aims of these textbooks are to help young pupils to acquire the essential knowledge about the life of the Buddha, his fundamental teaching and the historical development of Buddhism. The information is basically factual, although it places a marked emphasis on the salient character of Buddhist morality and its constructive attitude towards people and society.

Buddhism for Key Stage One provides an introduction to the basic concept of the Triple Gem, namely the Buddha, the Dharma and the Sangha. These three elements constitute the three pillars of Buddhism. The Buddha is the founder and teacher, the Dharma represents the Buddha's teachings, and the Sangha denotes the Buddhist community as a whole, living in accordance with the Buddha's teachings. In addition to these three elements covered in separate chapters, the textbook also includes ten selected Buddhist stories, which are to serve as additional aids to help the pupils gain a better grasp of Buddhist principles and see their application in various contexts.

The accompanying Pupil's Workbook contains various types of exercises based on standard teaching methods. They are intended for revision purposes and should be used at the discretion of the teacher. The English grammar and vocabulary are adapted to the level of an average pupil of Key Stage One. However, some pupils may need further assistance with the reading of this book. All Buddhist terms, printed in bold, are listed in the glossary.

The subjects covered in this and the remaining issues of this series are in accordance with the syllabus prescribed in the UK by the revised National Curriculum in 1994.

This textbook is produced by the Buddhist Education Foundation. It is a charitable organisation which aims to promote the education of Buddhism in this country.

The authors of the text are Jing Yin and Ken Hudson. Jing Yin is a Buddhist monk from China. He studied Buddhism in China and Sri Lanka. Currently he is in his final year of his Ph.D. programme at the School of Oriental and African Studies, University of London. He is being supervised by Dr T. Skorupski, who has also been consulted in matters relating to this textbook. Ken Hudson has taught in Australia, Canada and England for more than 20 years. Liu Yanfeng, a professional artist, has done the illustrations.

We would appreciate receiving feedback from both teachers and pupils about this first edition with a view to improving the material for the next edition

President
The Buddhist Education Foundation (UK)

CONTENTS

THE BUDDHA

Tian Tan Buddha Statue in Po Lin Monastery Hong Kong

Buddhism is the teachings of the **Buddha**. He was a wise teacher. His teachings help people to live wisely and happily. Today, more than 500 million people in the world follow his teachings. In this unit, we are going to tell you the story of the Buddha.

About 2,600 years ago, there lived a great king named **Suddhodana**. He had a pretty wife called **Maya**. They lived at the bottom of the Himalayas Mountains in northern India.

One night, Queen Maya had a wonderful dream. She saw a huge white elephant come into her room. It was holding a lotus flower. The elephant blew its trunk as it was walking round her bed three times.

In the morning, the king asked his wise men about the queen's dream. They said, "*Oh King! A great son will be born to Queen Maya.*" The king and queen were very happy with this news.

Queen Maya gave birth to Prince **Siddhartha** in a pretty royal park. It was the full-moon day of May. All the trees were in flower. The bees were humming around the fresh flowers. The birds were singing sweetly. Everyone was happy because a prince had been born.

The prince was very kind. He never hurt anything, not even the smallest animals.

One day, his cousin shot a swan. It fell to the ground and was badly hurt. The prince felt sorry for it. He picked it up and looked after it. He knew that all animals wanted to live. They did not want to die.

In the palace, the prince had many teachers. He was a very good student. His father wished that one day he would become a great king.

The prince grew up to be a strong, handsome, young man.
He married a beautiful girl. They lived happily together.

One day, when the prince visited a village, he saw four people: one sick, one old, one dead and a holy man. The first three made him very sad. The holy man made him think about what it meant to be happy.

At the age of twenty-nine, the prince gave up his palace life. He left his family to find a way to make everyone happy.

For the next six years, he went from place to place. He learn from many wise teachers. He had a lot of hardship, but he did not give up. He kept looking for a way to get rid of sadness in the world. He became wiser day by day.

At last, he sat under a huge **Bodhi Tree**. He meditated over and over on these questions, "*Why do people suffer? How can I help them to be happy?*"

At the age of thirty-five, he found a way for people to end their pain and sadness. From then on, he was called the Buddha.

The Buddha first told his ideas to five monks, "*There are problems in all our lives. These problems come from being selfish. If we get rid of being selfish, we could be wise and happy.*"

For the next forty-five years, many people, rich and poor, young and old, came to listen to the Buddha's teachings, "*We should always think about what we do. If we do good, good things will happen to us. If we do bad, bad things will happen to us.*"

At the age of eighty, the Buddha passed away.

Unit 2

THE DHARMA

The main teachings of the Buddha are:

- ***DO NOT DO BAD***
- ***DO GOOD***
- ***KEEP YOUR MIND CLEAN***

Monks and nuns from Fa Yue Buddhist Monastery in Birmingham teaching Dharma to school children

Dharma is the teachings of the Buddha. It teaches us how to live wisely and happily. It tells us how to face and solve problems. When we follow the Dharma, it brings much happiness and peace.

DO NOT DO BAD

Killing animals and being cruel to them is bad. Like us, animals do not want to get hurt. We should not harm them; not even just for fun.

DO NOT DO BAD

Stealing is bad. People who have their money or things stolen will be very sad. Those who steal will be punished for it.

DO NOT DO BAD

Telling lies is bad. Telling lies even for fun may get people into trouble. We should always tell the truth.

DO GOOD

We should respect our parents and teachers. They are ready to help us and give us good advice. They deserve our respect.

DO GOOD

We should help one another. Everyone needs help at times. Helping each other will make everybody happy.

We should make friends with good people. They will help us to become better people. It is best to keep away from people who do bad.

KEEP YOUR MIND CLEAN

Selfish thoughts make your mind unclean. When people are selfish, they only think about themselves. No one likes selfish people. We should not have selfish thoughts.

KEEP YOUR MIND CLEAN

Don't be greedy as it makes your mind unclean. When a greedy boy eats too much, he gets ill and feels terrible. In the same way, wanting too much of anything, such as toys and games, is not good for us. We should not have greedy thoughts.

KEEP YOUR MIND CLEAN

Angry thoughts make your mind unclean. When we lose our temper easily, we upset other people. Then no one wants to be our friend and we will be sad. So we should not have angry thoughts.

THE SANGHA

Monks and nuns from Amaravati Buddhist Monastery, Hemel Hempstead

The **Sangha** is a group of **monks** or **nuns**. They practise the Dharma. They hope that the Buddha's teachings can help to make people become happier and wiser. They want everyone to live a good and happy life.

Men can become monks. Monks usually get up at 5 o'clock in the morning. They study the Buddha's teachings after breakfast. Sometimes, they teach Dharma to people in the afternoon. In the evening, they meditate. They keep their minds clean and have kind hearts.

Women can become nuns. They also shave their heads. They usually wear robes of brown, yellow or grey. They live simple lives and work hard for the happiness of people. They are wise and cheerful, just like the monks.

Daddy is doing meditation, it helps him to relax after a hard day's work.

People who are not monks or nuns can also study the Buddha's teachings. They are called **lay people**. They respect the Buddha, the Dharma and the Sangha. They are friendly and peaceful to everybody.

If you get angry with someone who upsets you, then you will suffer even more yourself.

When lay people have problems, they go to monks and nuns for advice. To thank them for their good advice, lay people offer monks and nuns food and clothing as a sign of respect. They treat monks and nuns as special people.

Unit 4

THE TRIPLE GEM

The Buddha, the Dharma and the Sangha are called the **Triple Gem**. The Triple Gem is very special to Buddhists. They pay respect to the Buddha, learn the Dharma, and follow the advice of the Sangha. By doing this, Buddhists believe they can become wise and happy.

The Buddha is the first gem for Buddhists.

- *He is the founder of Buddhism.*
- *He found the Truth.*
- *He is the most honoured person in Buddhism.*
- *He represents wisdom.*
- *He taught us how to find happiness through wisdom and love.*

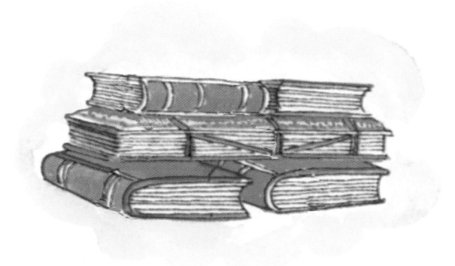

Sutras

The Dharma is the second gem for Buddhists.
- *It is the teachings of the Buddha.*
- *It shows the Truth.*
- *It helps us to gain happiness.*

The Sangha is the third gem for Buddhists.
 - *It is a group of monks or nuns.*
 - *It represents purity.*
 - *It sets a good example for Buddhists to follow.*

Unit 5
BUDDHIST STORIES

Some of the Buddha's teachings are very deep and difficult to understand. So when the Buddha was alive, he often used stories to help people to understand his teachings. The following ten stories will help you understand better his teachings in this book.

WILD DEER PARK
No killing

A long time ago, there was a beautiful forest. Many deer lived there. One day, a king took his men there to hunt. The king shot an arrow and hit a mother deer. She ran away in pain. Later the king found her hiding in some bushes with her baby deer. Even though she was bleeding and had tears in her eyes, she still fed her baby with milk. She soon died.

The king felt very sorry. He picked up the baby deer and said to it, "*I will now care for you.*" He then broke his bow in two. He said, "*I'll never hunt again.*"

To remember that day, he named the forest Wild Deer Park.

Like people, animals also have feelings. We should not kill them for fun or sport. It is unkind and selfish.

THE MOON IS LOOKING AT YOU
No stealing

Once there was a very poor family. They often went to their neighbour's garden to steal some vegetables.

One night, the father took along his little son into their neighbour's garden to steal some carrots. While the father was pulling out some carrots, his little boy stood beside him. Suddenly, his son whispered, "*Daddy, someone is looking at us.*"

The father became afraid. He quickly looked around but he could not see anyone. "*Where? Who?*" he asked.

The son pointed at the sky, "*There, Daddy. It's the moon. The moon is looking at us.*"

The father was shocked by what his son said. He thought that nobody could see what he was doing at night. His son's words made him feel ashamed.

He threw the carrots down and took his son by the hand. They both walked back home in the moonlight. After that he never stole anything again.

If we steal, people will know.

THE BUDDHA AND RAHULA
No lying

Rahula, the only son of the Buddha, became a monk. He was the youngest in the Sangha. All the monks loved and spoiled him. Rahula did whatever he liked. Sometimes he told lies just for the fun of it.

One day, the Buddha said to Rahula, "*Please bring me a basin of water. I want to wash my feet.*" He washed his feet in the basin of water and asked Rahula, "*Would you drink this water?*"

"*No, it's dirty!*" Rahula replied.

Then the Buddha asked Rahula to throw the water away.

The Buddha told Rahula, "*When water gets dirty, no one wants it. It is the same for those who tell lies, no one cares for them anymore.*"

Tears of shame came to Rahula's eyes. He never told another lie.

We should always tell the truth.

THE YOUNG DEER THAT PLAYED DEAD
Respecting teachers

A wise deer taught all the young deer how to escape from the hunters. One of them was a very good pupil. He was never bad in class. He also thanked the teacher after every lesson.

One day, this young deer was caught in a trap. The others ran away in fright. They ran to tell his mother. She cried when she heard about this.

The teacher comforted her, "*Don't worry. Your son is such a good pupil, he will come back safely.*"

As he was caught in the trap, the young deer remembered what the teacher had taught him. He pretended to be dead by sticking out his tongue and lying still. This made the hunter believe that the deer was really dead. When the hunter was preparing to cook the deer, it jumped up and ran away like the wind. His friends were so happy to see him back. They thanked the wise teacher for teaching him so well.

Being a good pupil brings great rewards.

THE BUDDHA THREADING THE NEEDLE

Helping each other

Anuruddha was a very good pupil, but he was blind. He did not feel sorry for himself because he was blind and kept up with his practice.

One day, he felt a hole in his robe. He tried to mend it, but found it very difficult. He could not even thread the needle. The Buddha came to his room to thread the needle for him. "*Who is threading the needle for me?*" Anuruddha asked.

"*It is the Buddha,*" the Buddha replied while he was mending the robe. Anuruddha felt really happy and was moved to tears.

Always help those who need it.

THE CRIPPLED & THE BLIND MEN

Helping each other

A crippled man and a blind man were left alone in a house. A fire broke out. Both were very scared. The blind man could not see the way out. The crippled man could not walk to it.

They decided to help each other. The blind man carried the crippled man on his back. The crippled man told the blind man where to go. Together, they got out of the burning house.

If we help each other, we will all win.

THE FISHMONGER'S
Making good friends

The Buddha and **Ananda** were begging in a city. They passed a fishmonger's. The Buddha said, "*Ananda, touch the rope where the fish are hanging and smell your fingers.*"

Ananda did this and said, "*It smells awful !*"

The Buddha said, "*This is the same with making friends, if you mix with bad people, you will become bad. This is like the smell from the rope in the fishmonger's.*"

Next, they passed a spice shop. The Buddha said, "*Ananda, touch the spice wrapper and then smell your fingers.*"

Ananda did this and said, "*My fingers smell very nice.*"

The Buddha said, "*This is the same with making friends. If you mix with good people, you will be a good person. This is like the nice smell you got from the spice wrappers.*"

If you mix with good and honest people, you will be a good person. If you mix with lazy and bad people, you will be a bad person.

Now, it smells very nice!

THE FOX AND THE OTTERS

Do not be selfish

A fox's wife wanted to eat some fresh fish. The fox tried to find some for her near the river. He saw two otters at the river dragging along a big fish. Both wanted the best parts of the fish. The fox watched them for a short time. Then he went up to ask if he could divide the fish for them. The otters were delighted.

The fox divided the fish into three pieces. He gave the head to one otter and the tail to the other. While the otters were thinking how the fox would divide the best part of the fish, the fox ran away with it. The otters had only themselves to blame for being so selfish.

Do not be selfish, share with others.

THE SNAKE'S HEAD AND TAIL

Do not fight with each other

The snake's tail had a fight with its head. The tail said, "*You have led me for so long. Now it's time for me to lead you.*"

The head said, "*I should be the leader. I have eyes and a mouth.*"

The tail said, "*You need me to move. Without me, you can't go anywhere.*"

Then the tail grabbed a tree branch and would not let go. The snake's head gave up and let the tail be the leader. The head did not want to help the tail. The tail could not see where it was going. Then, it fell into a fire pit. The snake was burnt to death.

It hurts both sides when you quarrel.

THE CLEANING WOMAN
Clean mind

A woman worked very hard cleaning the streets. As her clothes were dirty and smelly, all the people ran away from her when they saw her. When the Buddha talked to her nicely, the people were surprised.

Run! Run!
She really smells!

They asked the Buddha, "*You always ask us to be clean. Why are you talking to this smelly woman?*"

The Buddha replied, "*Although this woman is smelly, her mind is clean. She is polite and she works hard for others. Some people look clean and tidy, but their minds are full of bad thoughts!*"

Having a clean mind is more important than wearing clean clothes.

GLOSSARY

Ananda	a monk who had a good memory
Anuruddha	a monk who went blind
Bodhi Tree	the tree under which Prince Siddhartha became the Buddha
Buddha	a wise teacher
Dharma	the teachings of the Buddha
Lay people	Buddhists who are not monks and nuns
Maya	the Buddha's mother
Monk	a male Buddhist who has left home to live and practise in a monastery
Nun	a female Buddhist who has left home to live and practise in a nunnery
Rahula	the Buddha's son
Sangha	a group of Buddhist monks or nuns
Siddhartha	the name of the prince before he became the Buddha
Suddhodana	the Buddha's father
Sutras	talks given by the Buddha
Triple Gem	the Buddha, the Dharma and the Sangha

INDEX

BIBLIOGRAPHY

Conze, E. *Buddhism: Its Essence and Development*. London, Harper Torchbooks, 1975.

Conze, E. *A Short History of Buddhism*. Oxford, 1993.

Rahula, W. *What the Buddha Taught*. London, 1978.

Warder, A. K. *Indian Buddhism*. Delhi, Motilal Banarsidass, 1980.

Wijayaratna, M. *Buddhist Monastic Life according to the texts of the Theravada Tradition*. Cambridge, 1990.

BUDDHISM

KEY STAGE 1

By

Jing Yin
Ken Hudson

Published by
Buddhist Education Foundation (UK)
Registered Charity No.: 1073008
2000

First published in Great Britain in 2002
by
Buddhist Education Foundation (UK)
Second print , August 2003

This is a complimentary Buddhist textbook,
which can be obtained from
The Buddhist Education Foundation (UK)
BCM 9459 London WC1N 3XX
United Kingdom

WWW.buddhisteducation.co.uk
info@buddhisteducation.co.uk

Registered Charity No.: 1073008

ISBN 0 9536928 0 0

Illustrated by Yanfeng Liu
Produced by media 2000

INTRODUCTION

This workbook is an integral part of the Buddhism Key Stage 1 course, and is strongly recommended for use in conjunction with the relevant textbook. Unit numbers have been included throughout the workbook, indicating the corresponding units in the textbook. The aim of this workbook is to reinforce the understanding of Buddhist concepts, Buddhist vocabulary and the life of the Buddha.

Some general strategies are suggested below in order to facilitate an effective use of this workbook:

1) Examine and discuss the drawings before the students attempt to read the accompanying pages.

2) Make the students aware of the new and difficult words when they read each section - these include both Buddhist terms and general English words.

3) Having read the relevant pages in the textbook with the students, go through the corresponding activities in the workbook.

4) Ensure that all activities for each unit are completed before moving on to the next unit.

5) Let the students go through the activities in groups rather than individually.

6) Discuss with the students their views on important moral concepts that arise during the process.

ACTIVITIES

1. Join part A with part B to make proper sentences:

A	B
a) Buddhism is the teachings of	a wise teacher.
b) The Buddha was	Buddhists.
c) The Buddha's teachings help people to	the Buddha.
d) Today, there are over 500 million people who are	live wisely and happily.

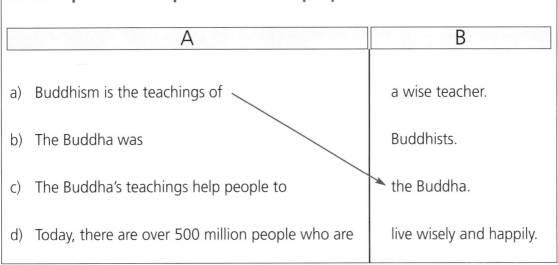

2. Complete the following sentences. Choose the correct answer from the list:

| elephant   India   ~~2,600 years~~   lotus   Queen Maya   Himalayas |

a) About _2,600 years_ ago, there lived a great teacher.

b) The Buddha lived near the _____ mountains in northern _____ .

c) The Buddha's mother was called _____ .

d) Queen Maya had a dream. It was about a huge white _____ ,

which was carrying a _____ flower.

3. Complete the following sentences. Choose the correct answer from the list:

| son   birth   Siddhartha   bees   happy   ~~wise~~   Queen   full-moon   birds |

a) In the morning, the king asked his ____wise____ men about the queen's dream.

They said, "Oh King! A great _____ will be born to _____ Maya.

"The king and queen were very _____ with this news.

b) Queen Maya gave birth to Prince _____ in a pretty royal park.

It was the _____ day of May. All the trees were in flower.

The _____ were humming around the fresh flowers.

The _____ were singing sweetly. Every animal was happy with the

_____ of the prince.

4. Work out the following jumbled words from the list below:

| Bodhi Tree   Siddhartha   Maya   Buddha   holy man   ~~lotus~~ |

a) sltuo _____*lotus*_____ d) oyhl amn _____

b) yaMa _____ e) dBiho eTre _____

c) ihrtdSahda _____ f) adBhdu _____

5. Colour in the drawing of the birth of Prince Siddhartha:

6. Answers these questions using the words in the list below:

thirty-five	six	Bodhi Tree	prince's cousin	twenty-nine	elephant
	eighty	~~2,600 years~~	May	Queen Maya	four

a) How many years ago was the Buddha born? _2,600 years_

b) What is the name of the mother of the Buddha? _____

c) Which animal did Queen Maya see in her dream? _____

d) In which month was the Buddha born? _____

e) Who shot the swan that the prince saved? _____

f) How many signs did the prince see? _____

g) How old was the prince when he left his palace? _____

h) How many years of hardship did the prince suffer? _____

i) What is the name of the tree where the prince meditated? _____

j) How old was the prince when he found a way to end the sadness of all people? _____

k) How old was the Buddha when he passed away? _____

7. Rearrange the words to make proper sentences:

a) was Siddhartha. named prince The

The prince was named Siddhartha.

b) wanted all to animals The live. prince

_____

c) a prince young strong, The handsome, man. was

_____

d) prince to The make happy. wanted everyone

_____

e) meditated The a under tree. Bodhi prince

_____

f) told his first Buddha ideas to monks. The five

_____

g) passed The at age of away eighty. Buddha the

_____

Unit 2

ACTIVITIES

---

1. Join part A with part B to make proper sentences:

A	B
a) The Dharma	make your mind unclean.
b) Killing animals	to respect your parents and teachers.
c) It is good	keep away from doing bad.
d) We should	is the teachings of the Buddha.
e) Selfish thoughts	is bad.

---

2. Complete the following sentences. Choose the correct answer from the list:

honest ~~Dharma~~ parents bad animals

a) Learning _____*Dharma*_____ will bring you much happiness.

b) You should never harm _____ for any reason.

c) Stealing is _____ .

d) It is always better to be _____ .

e) It is good to respect your _____ .

3. Complete the following sentences. Choose the correct answer from the list:

thoughts   unclean   peace   ill   happily   games

problems   greedy   ~~teachings~~

a)   Dharma is the _____*teachings*_____ of the Buddha. It tells us how to live wisely

and _____ . It teaches us how to face and solve _____ .

When we follow the Dharma, it brings much happiness and _____ .

b)   Greedy thoughts make your mind _____ . When a boy is

_____ and eats too much, he will get _____ . Then he suffers. In

the same way, wanting too much of anything, such as toys and _____

is not good for us. We should not have greedy _____ .

4. Draw different coloured lines from A to B to show opposite actions:

A) BAD ACTIONS	B) GOOD ACTIONS
a) killing animals	being honest
b) stealing	helping others
c) telling lies	sharing with others
d) being selfish	making friends
e) being angry	having a calm mind
f) fighting with people	respecting your parents
g) shouting back at your parents	being kind to all animals
h) walking past an injured person	respecting other people's things

5. Work out the following jumbled words from the list below:

| killing | greed | ~~Dharma~~ | angry | stealing | honest | selfish | respect |

a) mhaDar ___*Dharma*___

b) lnlikig _____

c) hefsils _____

d) tsgalien _____

e) ohetsn _____

f) erecpts _____

g) rdege _____

h) gynra _____

6. Place the following in the correct column under "DOING GOOD" or "DOING BAD":

fighting   killing   helping others   lying   sharing   making friends
selfishness   not helping others   staying calm   respecting teachers
greely   stealing   ~~kindness to animals~~   honesty

A) DOING GOOD	B) DOING BAD
Kindness to animals _____	_____
_____	_____
_____	_____
_____	_____
_____	_____
_____	_____

7. Rearrange the words to make proper sentences:

a)   teachings. is the The Dharma Buddha's
     The Dharma is Buddha's teachings
     _____

b)   harm should We animals. not

     _____

c)   steal. not should We

     _____

d)   should tell We lies. not

     _____

e)   our respect parents. should We

     _____

f)   help each should other. We

     _____

g)   friends good with people. make should We

     _____

h)   should We keep away doing bad. from

     _____

i)   not should selfish. We be

     _____

j)   be not greedy. should We

     _____

k)   not We angry. be should

     _____

ACTIVITIES

1. **Join part A with part B to make proper sentences:**

A	B
a) The Sangha is	monks.
b) Women can become	Buddhists.
c) Men can become	a group of monks and nuns.
d) People who follow Buddhism are	nuns.

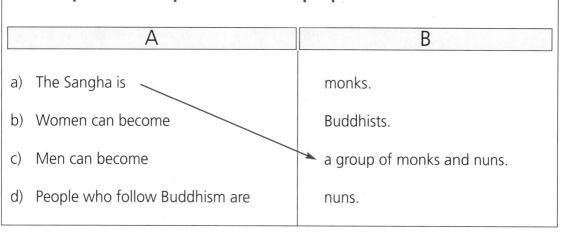

2. **Complete the following sentences. Choose the correct answer from the list:**

> monks   minds   happy   ~~Sangha~~   nuns   teachings

a) The ___*Sangha*___ is always ready to explain the Buddha's teachings to people.

b) The Sangha hopes that the Buddha's _____ can help to make people become happier.

c) The Sangha wants everyone to live a good and _____ life.

d) The Sangha has clean _____ and kind hearts.

e) Women can become _____ .

f) Men can become _____ .

3. Work out the following jumbled words from the list below:

| nun | Sangha | ~~lay people~~ | monk | robes | meditate |

a) lya pploee ___*lay people*___

b) nnu _____

c) ahnaSg _____

d) eemittda _____

e) onmk _____

f) bsroe _____

4. Complete the following sentences. Choose the correct answer from the list:

| kind | ~~monks~~ | respect | lay people | advice | peaceful |
| problems | food | Buddha's |

a) People who are not ___*monks*___ or nuns can also study the _____

teachings. They are called _____ . They are _____ and

gentle people. They are friendly and _____ to everybody.

b) When lay people have _____ , they go to monks and nuns for

advice. To thank them for their good _____ , lay people offer monks

and nuns _____ and clothing. They have great _____ for the

monks and nuns.

5. Answers these questions using the words in the list below:

grey	Sangha	woman	meditate	for advice	wise	give food

a) What name is given to a group of monks and nuns? _____*Sangha*_____

b) Give one word to describe a monk/nun. _____

c) Monk is to man as nun is to? _____

d) Name a colour a monk/nun's robe can be? _____

e) What does a monk/nun do in the evenings? _____

f) Why do lay people go to see a monk/nun? _____

g) Give one way lay people help monks/nuns. _____

6. Rearrange the words to make proper sentences:

a)   monks Sangha nuns. The or is

_____

b)   Sangha happy. everyone wants to The be

_____

c)   life. lives Sangha a The simple

_____

d)   and Sangha The is peaceful. wise

_____

e)   can Women nuns. become

_____

f)   become Men monks. can

_____

g)   people gentle. are Lay and kind

_____

7. Colour in the drawings of a monk and a nun:

ACTIVITIES

---

1. Join part A with part B to make proper sentences:

A	B
a) The Triple Gem is very special to	wisdom.
b) The first Gem is	Buddhists.
c) The second Gem is	the Sangha.
d) The third Gem is	purity.
e) The Buddha represents	the Dharma.
f) Dharma represents	the Buddha.
g) The Sangha represents	truth.

---

2. Complete the following sentences. Choose the correct answer from the list:

teachings   Buddha   Buddhists   ~~Triple Gem~~   Buddhism

a) The Buddha, the Dharma and the Sangha are called the _____*Triple Gem*_____.

b) The Triple Gem is very special in _____.

c) The _____ is the founder of Buddhism.

d) The Dharma is the _____ of the Buddha.

e) The Sangha sets a good example for _____ to follow.

3. Complete the following sentences. Choose the correct answer from the list:

| happy | advice | ~~Triple Gem~~ | Dharma | Buddha |

The ___Triple Gem___ is very special for Buddhists. They pay respect to the

_____, learn the _____, and follow the _____ of

the Sangha. By doing this, the Buddhists believe they can become wise and

_____.

4. Work out the following jumbled words from the list below:

| Dharma | ~~purity~~ | Triple Gem | Sangha | Buddha | wisdom | truth |

a) ruiytp _____*Purity*_____   e) ngaaSh _____

b) urtth _____   f) udBdah _____

c) hDaamr _____   g) isdwmo _____

d) rTielp eGm _____

5. Answers these questions using the words in the list below:

| The Sangha | The Buddha | ~~The Triple Gem~~ | The Dharma |
| | a group of monks or nuns | The Dharma | The Buddha |

a) What is the Buddha, the Dharma and the Sangha called? _The Triple Gem_

b) What is the first Gem? _____

c) What is the second Gem? _____

d) What is the third Gem? _____

e) Who was the founder of Buddhism? _____

f) What is Buddha's teachings called? _____

g) Who are the Sangha? _____

6. Pick two words from the list below, which go with each of the three Gems:

| truth | wisdom | ~~The Buddha~~ | The Sangha | purity | The Dharma |

a) First Gem _The Buddha_ _____

b) Second Gem_____ _____

c) Third Gem_____ _____

ACTIVITIES

Here are some questions to answer about the story you have just read.

Talk over each question with a friend. Write your answer in a short sentence.

WILD DEER PARK
No killing

1) What lived in the beautiful forest?

_____

_____

2) What did the king do in the forest?

_____

_____

3) How did the king feel when he saw the dead mother deer and her baby?

_____

_____

4) Why did the king break his bow?

_____

_____

5) Why did the king give the park a special name?

_____

_____

6) Why is it important not to kill animals for sport or fun?

_____

_____

THE MOON IS LOOKING AT YOU
No stealing

1) Why did the father steal vegetables?

_____

_____

2) Which vegetable was the father trying to steal?

_____

3) Why did the son point at the sky?

_____

_____

4) Why did the father feel sad?

_____

_____

5) What could the father have said the next day to the friend whose vegetables he was stealing?

_____

_____

6) Should all people who steal be punished?

_____

_____

THE BUDDHA AND RAHULA
No lying

1 What is the name of the Buddha's son?

_____

2 Why was Rahula spoilt by older monks?

_____

3 After the Buddha had washed his feet, what was in the basin?

_____

_____

4 What did the Buddha tell Rahula the dirty water meant?

_____

_____

5 Why did Rahula have tears of shame?

_____

_____

6 Why is it important to always be honest?

_____

THE YOUNG DEER THAT PLAYED DEAD
Respecting teachers

1   Two reasons are given in the story why one of the deer was a
    good student. What are the reasons?

    _____

    _____

2   Why did the wise deer teach the young deer?

    _____

    _____

3   How did the young deer feel when he was caught in the trap?

    _____

    _____

4   Why did the teacher tell the young deer's mother that he'd come back safely?

    _____

    _____

5   How did the young deer pretend to be dead?

    _____

    _____

6   Why is it important to listen to your teachers and parents?

    _____

THE BUDDHA THREADING THE NEEDLE
Helping each other

1   What was the matter with Anuruddha?

_____

_____

2   What was the problem with Anuruddha's robe?

_____

_____

3   What did Anuruddha find hard to do when he was trying to mend his robe?

_____

_____

4   Why did the Buddha help Anuruddha?

_____

_____

5   Why did Anuruddha start to cry?

_____

_____

6   Why is it important to help those who are less fortunate than ourselves?

_____

_____

THE CRIPPLED AND THE BLIND MEN
Helping each other

1   What was the matter with the two men?

_____

_____

2   Why were both of the two men scared?

_____

_____

3   How did the blind man and the crippled man help each other to

escape the fire?

_____

_____

4   Why is it important to help each other?

_____

_____

THE FISHMONGER'S
Making good friends

1   Who were begging in a city?

_____

_____

2   Why did the Buddha ask Ananda to touch the rope in the fish shop?

_____

_____

3   Why did the Buddha ask Ananda to touch the wrapper in the spice shop?

_____

_____

4   What did the rope from the fish shop mean?

_____

_____

5   What did the wrapper from the spice shop mean?

_____

_____

THE FOX AND THE OTTERS
Do not be selfish

1   Why did the fox go to the river?

_____

2   Whom did the fox meet at the river?

_____

_____

3   Why did the two otters both want the best part of the fish?

_____

_____

4   Why did the fox offer to divide the fish for the otters?

_____

_____

5   Why did the fox bite off the head and the tail of the fish and
    give them to the otters?

_____

_____

6   Why is it important to share whatever you have with others?

_____

_____

THE SNAKE'S HEAD AND TAIL
Do not fight with each other

1   What did the snake's tail have a fight with?

_____

2   Why did the tail want to be the leader?

_____

3   Why didn't the head want to give up being the leader?

_____

4   What did the snake's tail grab hold of?

_____

_____

5   Why didn't the head help the tail?

_____

_____

6   What happened to the snake in the end?

_____

_____

7   Why is it important NOT to fight?

_____

_____

THE CLEANING WOMAN
Clean mind

1   Why did the people run away from the woman who cleaned their streets?

_____

_____

2   Describe the woman who cleaned the streets.

_____

_____

3   Why was the woman important to the city?

_____

_____

4   Why did the Buddha say : "Some people look clean and tidy,
     but their minds are full of bad thoughts?"

_____

_____

5   Why is it important NOT to judge people only by their looks?

_____

_____

B	C	F	G	P	U	R	I	T	Y	Z	B	G	Q	W	A	Q	B	V
U	B	Q	V	W	K	T	D	W	I	S	D	O	M	L	B	K	O	Y
M	C	U	Z	B	A	R	K	H	C	Y	U	Z	O	U	G	V	D	A
E	B	K	D	G	Q	U	C	N	A	Q	A	T	M	A	Y	A	H	U
D	Q	Y	V	D	Y	T	C	U	Y	R	U	K	Z	S	C	V	I	K
I	K	G	W	A	H	H	K	N	K	S	M	C	U	A	U	G	T	Y
T	M	O	N	K	V	A	V	S	G	F	B	A	V	N	Z	Y	R	Q
A	C	S	I	D	D	H	A	R	T	H	A	Q	W	G	B	K	E	A
T	B	L	A	Y	P	E	O	P	L	E	K	G	Y	H	V	Z	E	V
E	A	C	W	T	R	I	P	L	E	G	E	M	U	A	W	G	A	Q

WORD SEARCH ONE: BUDDHIST WORDS

Help me find these words. They are written up, down and at an angle. Highlight each word when you find it. Use each letter once only. The first one has been done for you:

~~BODHI TREE~~	MAYA	SANGHA
BUDDHA	MEDITATE	SIDDHARTHA
DHARMA	MONK	TRIPLE GEM
LAY PEOPLE	NUNS	TRUTH
LOTUS	PURITY	WISDOM

S	Y	P	V	Q	S	W	Y	Q	R	L	Q	M	E	V	U	B	P	W
I	W	U	U	A	R	T	V	A	L	O	R	E	Z	D	G	D	U	S
Q	D	D	H	R	I	T	M	H	A	T	U	S	S	W	I	D	Z	V
T	S	V	T	Z	V	S	H	D	U	Y	T	U	P	T	D	P	Q	D
R	U	T	H	A	U	I	D	A	L	U	P	T	A	W	D	H	A	H
T	R	H	S	W	N	Q	H	A	A	E	S	W	R	T	E	H	A	H
R	I	P	N	U	G	G	H	D	O	P	Q	I	Z	A	M	R	M	U
D	A	L	Z	D	N	S	D	D	G	P	I	T	S	S	P	O	M	A
H	Z	E	A	S	M	U	B	P	S	H	L	Q	R	D	O	M	N	Y
A	R	M	G	E	G	S	B	O	D	V	U	E	Z	E	E	K	A	Z

WORD SEARCH TWO: BUDDHIST WORDS

Help me find these words. They follow the shape of a snake's body. Highlight each word when you find it. Use each letter once only. The first one has been done for you:

BUDDHISM

BUDDHA

SIDDHARTHA

MAYA

MEDITATE

LAY PEOPLE

PURITY

MONK

WISDOM

NUNS

DHARMA

LOTUS

SANGHA

BODHI TREE

TRUTH

TRIPLE GEM

SUTRAS

RAHULA

NAME OF SPONSOR

助 印 功 德 芳 名

Document Serial No : 96003

委印文號：96003

Book Title:BUDDHISM KEY STAGE I & WORKBOOK FOR KEY STAGE 1

英文佛教教科書（第一冊）及作業簿 合刊

Book Serial No., 書號：EN168

N.T.Dollars :

200,000：鄭六海（迴向十方法界眾生，宿世冤親債主，解冤釋結，業障消除，福慧雙修；
並願身體健康，闔家平安）。

4,000：陳光雄設計規劃有限公司。林于甄。

1,000：王林明如。

191,000：佛陀教育基金會。

Total: N.T. Dollars: 400,000 ; 10,000 copies.
以上合計：台幣 400,000 元；恭印 10,000 冊。

DEDICATION OF MERIT

May the merit and virtue
accrued from this work
adorn Amitabha Buddha's Pure Land,
repay the four great kindnesses above,
and relieve the suffering of
those on the three paths below.

May those who see or hear of these efforts
generate Bodhi-mind,
spend their lives devoted to the Buddha Dharma,
and finally be reborn together in
the Land of Ultimate Bliss.
Homage to Amita Buddha!

NAMO AMITABHA

南 無 阿 彌 陀 佛

【BUDDHISM KEY STAGE I & WORKBOOK FOR KEY STAGE 1
英文佛教教科書（第一冊）及作業簿 合刊】

財團法人佛陀教育基金會 印贈

台北市杭州南路一段五十五號十一樓

Printed and donated for free distribution by

The Corporate Body of the Buddha Educational Foundation

11F., 55 Hang Chow South Road Sec 1, Taipei, Taiwan, R.O.C.

Tel: 886-2-23951198 , Fax: 886-2-23913415

Email: overseas@budaedu.org

Website:http://www.budaedu.org

This book is strictly for free distribution, it is not for sale.

Printed in Taiwan

10,000 copies; March 2007

EN168-6395

美國淨宗學會

AMITABHA BUDDHIST SOCIETY OF U.S.A.

650 S. BERNARDO AVENUE

SUNNYVALE, CA 94087, U.S.A.

TEL: (408)736-3386   FAX: (408)736-3389

http://www.amtb-usa.org